herbs & spices

Published by:
TYPHOON MEDIA CORPORATION

herbs & spices

Herbs & Spices
© TYPHOON MEDIA CORPORATION

Publisher
Simon St. John Bailey

Editor-in-chief
Susan Knightley

Prepress
Precision Prep & Press

Includes Index
ISBN 9781582797335
UPC 615269973318

2010

Printed in The United States

introduction

Herbs are among the oldest of ingredients used
to add interest and flavor to food. The use
of herbs in cooking can be traced back
to the earliest years of man's existence.
Spices have a mystic all of their own. Associated
with the exotic, wars have been fought over them,
men have died in their quest and in past times
spices have been used in place
of gold and money. While today

they may be considered inexpensive and an everyday commodity, there is no denying that a pinch of chili, a grind of pepper or a teaspoon of ginger will add that special touch to a dish.

This book packed with aromatic suggestions presents you with delights to suit any occasion. Here you will find an exciting collection of recipes that show you just how easy herbs and spices are to use. So whether it's a delicately flavored soup, a robust pasta plate or the all-time favorite pizza, you are sure to find what you are looking for in our fragrant selection.

Storing Herbs

• Most fresh herbs will keep for about a week if stored correctly in the refrigerator. Placing the herbs in a jar of water and covering with a plastic food bag, then

sealing the bag around the jar is probably
the method that will keep herbs fresh
for the longest period of time.

- To dry herbs is inexpensive and easy. The
  simplest method is to tie the herbs in small
  loose bunches and to hang them upside-
  down in an airy place. Once dried, remove
  the leaves from the stems and place in
  airtight containers. Always store dried herbs
  in a cool dark place.

Grinding Spices

- Dry-frying whole spices before grinding
  mellows the flavor and will enhance your
  cooking. To dry-fry spices, heat a heavy-
  based frying pan over a medium heat.
  Add spices and stir constantly until they
  are evenly browned. Be careful not to let
  the spices burn. Remove from the pan
  and allow to cool before grinding.

- The traditional pestle and mortar is ideal
  for grinding spices and spice mixtures.
  A coffee grinder is also great for grinding
  spices, but do not use the same grinder as
  you use for coffee as the flavors will mix.

Difficulty scale

■□□I Easy to do

■■□I Requires attention

■■■I Requires experience

golden
butternut soup

■□□ I Cooking time: 35 minutes - Preparation time: 15 minutes

ingredients

- > **1 onion, chopped**
- > **1 clove garlic, crushed**
- > **4 cups/1 liter/1³/₄ pt chicken or vegetable stock**
- > **750 g/1¹/₂ lb butternut pumpkin, sliced**
- > **2 potatoes, sliced**
- > **¹/₂ teaspoon dried marjoram**
- > **¹/₂ teaspoon grated nutmeg**
- > **freshly ground black pepper**
- > **3 tablespoons buttermilk**
- > **snipped fresh chives to sprinkle**

method

1. Place onion, garlic and 2 tablespoons stock in a saucepan over a medium heat and cook for 2-3 minutes or until onion is soft.
2. Add remaining stock, pumpkin, potatoes, marjoram, nutmeg and black pepper to taste and cook, stirring occasionally, for 25 minutes, or until pumpkin and potato are tender.
3. Stir in buttermilk. Cool slightly. Purée soup, in batches, in a food processor or blender.
4. Return soup to a clean saucepan and heat gently, do not allow to boil or soup will curdle.
5. Pour soup into large mugs or warm bowls, sprinkle with snipped fresh chives and serve.

Serves 4

tip from the chef

This soup can be stored in the refrigerator for up to 3 days and reheated as required in a saucepan or in the microwave. In the microwave reheat the soup in the serving mugs. One serving will take 2-3 minutes to reheat on High (100%) –depending on the serving size.

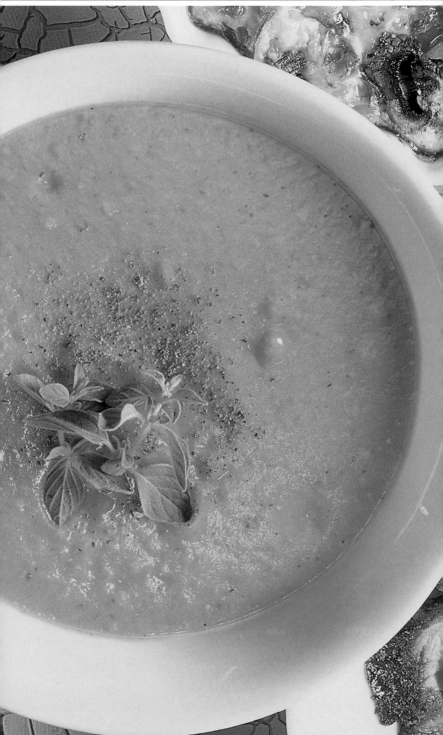

chilled
zucchini and dill soup

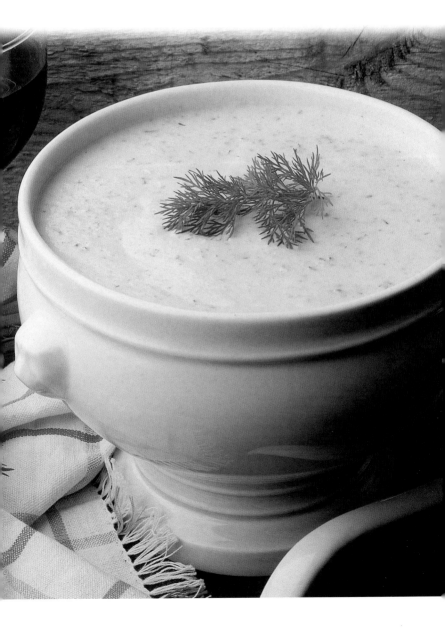

■ □ □ | Cooking time: 20 minutes - Preparation time: 5 minutes

method

1. Place stock, onion, zucchini, potato and cumin in a large saucepan. Bring to the boil over moderate heat, reduce heat and simmer for 20 minutes.
2. Blend or process soup mixture until smooth. Blend in cream.
3. Stir dill into the soup and chill for 3 hours in the refrigerator before serving.

Serves 4

ingredients

> 2 cups chicken stock
> 1 large onion, chopped
> 350 g/11 oz zucchini, chopped
> 1 large potato, chopped
> 1/2 teaspoon ground cumin
> 1 cup sour cream
> 2 tablespoons chopped fresh dill

tip from the chef

If you wish to get texture contrast, scatter croûtons over the soup. To make croûtons, cut bread in cubes, brush with olive oil, place in a baking tray and bake in a slow oven until dry and crispy.

herbed
creamy soups

■□□ | Cooking time: 55 / 40 minutes - Preparation time: 10 minutes each soup

ingredients

leek and parsnip soup
> 45 g/1¹/2 oz butter
> 2 leeks, sliced
> 750 g/1¹/2 lb parsnips, sliced
> 1 teaspoon finely grated orange rind
> 6 cups/1.5 liter/2¹/2 pt chicken stock
> freshly ground black pepper
> 2 tablespoons snipped fresh chives

roasted garlic and tomato soup
> 1 kg/2 lb Italian tomatoes, halved
> 5 cloves garlic, peeled
> 1 tablespoon olive oil
> salt and freshly ground black pepper
> 6 cups/1.5 liters/2¹/2 pt vegetable stock
> 1 large red onion, finely chopped
> 3 tablespoons chopped fresh basil

method

1. To make parsnip soup, heat butter in a saucepan, cook leeks for 5 minutes or until golden. Add parsnips, orange rind and 1 cup/250 ml/8 fl oz stock, cover, simmer for 15 minutes or until parsnips are soft. Stir in remaining stock and black pepper to taste, simmer for 30 minutes longer. Cool slightly.

2. Process soup in batches in a food processor or blender. Return soup to a clean pan, simmer for 5 minutes or until heated through. Sprinkle with chives and serve.

3. To make tomato soup, place tomatoes and garlic in a lightly greased baking tray, brush lightly with oil and sprinkle with salt and black pepper to taste. Bake at 190°C/375°F/Gas 5 for 30 minutes or until garlic is golden and tomatoes are soft. Cool slightly.

4. Process tomatoes, garlic and stock in batches until smooth. Place soup mixture and onion in a saucepan, simmer for 10 minutes or until heated through. Stir in basil and serve.

....
Serves 6 each soup

tip from the chef

Most soups freeze well and are good standbys for home or office lunches. Freeze in serving size portions and simply reheat in the microwave when required. Pack reheated soup in a vacuum flask and it will still be hot at lunch time.

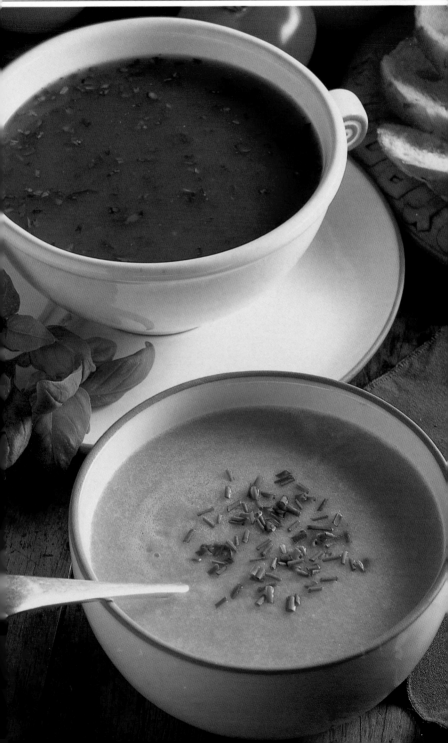

spicy corn
and lentil chowder

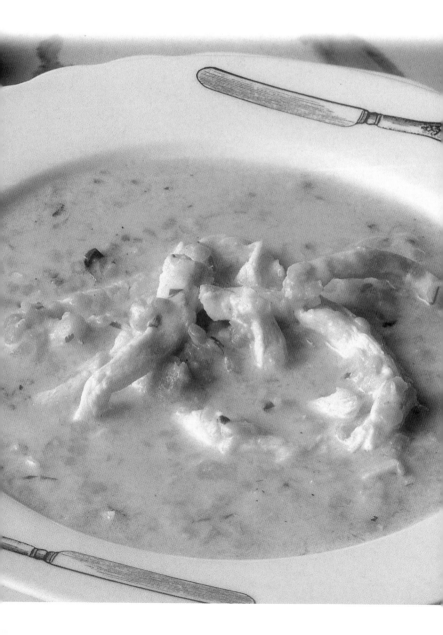

■□□ | Cooking time: 1 hour - Preparation time: 15 minutes

method

1. Bring a large saucepan of water to the boil. Add lentils, reduce heat and simmer for 12 minutes or until tender. Drain and set aside.
2. Melt butter in a saucepan over a medium heat, add garlic, onion, chili, cardamom and cumin and cook, stirring, for 3 minutes or until onion is soft.
3. Add lentils, stock, coconut milk, chicken and sweet corn and bring to the boil. Reduce heat and simmer for 45 minutes. Sprinkle with coriander and serve.

....
Serves 6

ingredients

> 200 g/7 oz red lentils
> 30 g/1 oz butter
> 2 cloves garlic, crushed
> 1 onion, chopped
> 1 small fresh green chili, chopped
> 1 teaspoon ground cardamom
> 1 teaspoon ground cumin
> 2 cups/500 ml/16 fl oz vegetable stock
> 1 1/2 cups/375 ml/ 12 fl oz coconut milk
> 250 g/8 oz cooked chicken, chopped
> 375 g/12 oz canned creamed sweet corn
> 3 tablespoons chopped fresh coriander

tip from the chef

One of the simplest soups you can make for a hearty and economical family meal.

barbecue
herb ricotta

■□□ I Cooking time: 20 minutes - Preparation time: 10 minutes

ingredients
> **750 g/1¹/₂ lb fresh ricotta cheese, in one piece**
> **2 tablespoons olive oil**
> **2 tablespoons paprika**
> **2 tablespoons chopped fresh marjoram**
> **2 tablespoons chopped fresh parsley**
> **freshly ground black pepper**

method
1. Place ricotta cheese on a wire rack and set aside to drain for 1 hour. Transfer ricotta cheese to a baking tray and brush with olive oil. Combine paprika, marjoram, parsley and black pepper to taste and sprinkle over ricotta.
2. Cook ricotta cheese in preheated hot kettle barbecue for 20 minutes or until golden. Alternatively, cover tray with aluminum foil and cook on the barbecue grill or bake in the oven at 180°C/350°F/Gas 4.

....
Serves 6

tip from the chef
This recipe is a great starter for outdoor barbecues or, when served with a crisp green salad, a novel light luncheon dish. Fresh ricotta cheese is available from delicatessens. Take care when handling as it is quite fragile, however once baked it becomes firm.

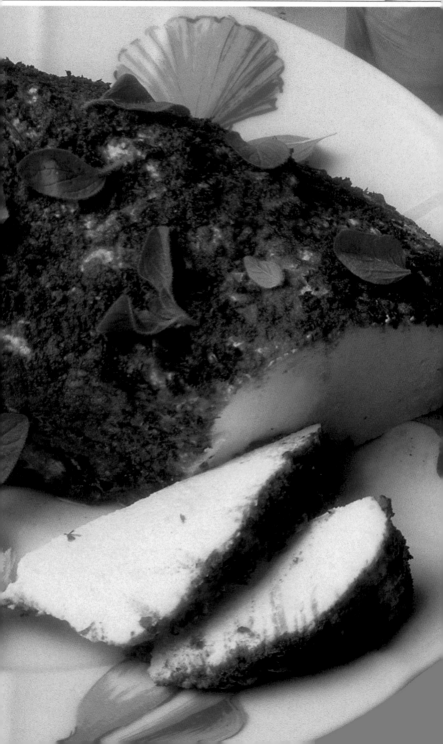

coriander
bean salad

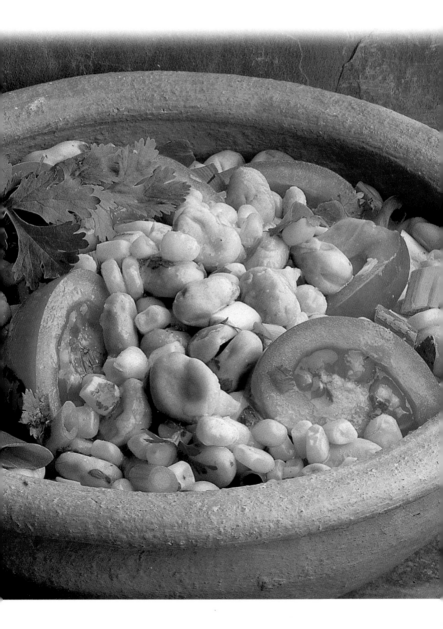

■☐☐ | Cooking time: 35 minutes - Preparation time: 15 minutes

method

1. Boil, steam or microwave broad beans and sweet corn, separately, until tender.
2. Place hot broad beans, sweet corn, tomatoes, spring onions and coriander in a bowl.
3. To make dressing, place oil, lemon juice, cumin and black pepper to taste in a screwtop jar and shake well to combine. Pour over bean mixture and toss to combine.
4. Set aside, tossing occasionally, until beans are cool before serving.

Serves 8

ingredients

> 500 g/1 lb shelled fresh broad beans or frozen broad beans
> 250 g/8 oz fresh or frozen sweet corn kernels
> 4 tomatoes, cut into wedges
> 6 spring onions, chopped
> 2 tablespoons chopped fresh coriander

cumin dressing

> 1/4 cup/60 ml/2 fl oz olive oil
> 1/4 cup/60 ml/2 fl oz lemon juice
> 1/2 teaspoon ground cumin
> freshly ground black pepper

tip from the chef

All parts of the coriander plant can be used. However you should be aware that if a recipe calls for fresh coriander you should not substitute it for the dried seeds or ground coriander (this is ground coriander seeds not leaf), as the two have completely different flavors.

pickled
grapes

■□□ | Cooking time: 10 minutes - Preparation time: 15 minutes

ingredients

> 1.5 kg/3 lb mixed black and green grapes
> 3¹/2 cups apple cider vinegar
> 3¹/2 cups water
> 200 g/6¹/2 oz brown sugar
> 1 tablespoon salt
> 2 teaspoons whole cloves
> 4 cinnamon sticks, broken into pieces

method

1. Wash grapes and break into small bunches. Discard any over-ripe or damaged grapes, and pack bunches into four wide mouthed 1-liter/4-cup jars or two 2-liter/8-cup jars.
2. Place vinegar, water, sugar, salt, cloves and cinnamon into a large saucepan and bring to the boil. Reduce heat and simmer for 8 minutes, set aside and cool to room temperature.
3. Pour liquid into each jar, making sure to fill to the top. Seal jars and set aside for 2 weeks at room temperature, then store in a cool place.

Makes about 8 cups

tip from the chef

Excellent to team with assorted cheeseboards. Complete with wholemeal bread and green leaves.

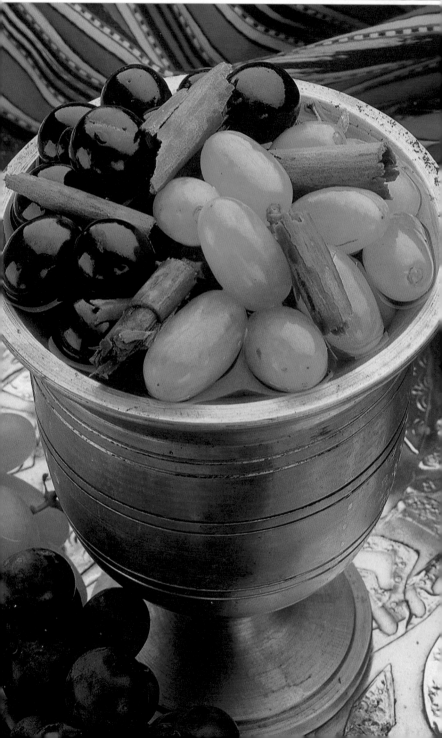

summer
vegetables with aioli

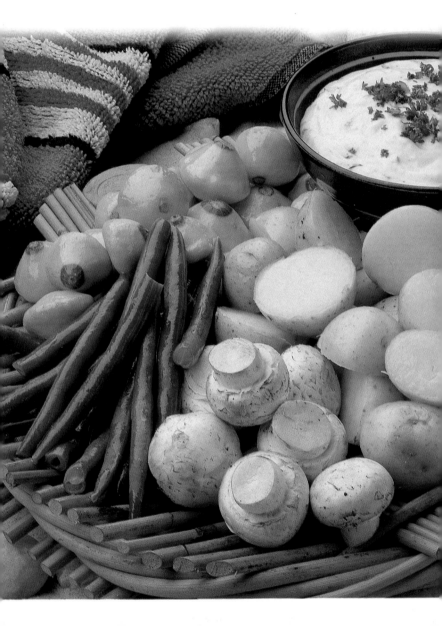

◼◻◻ | Cooking time: 30 minutes - Preparation time: 20 minutes

method

1. Boil, steam or microwave asparagus, squash, beans and potatoes, separately, until just tender. Drain, then refresh under cold running water.
2. To make aioli, place egg yolks, lemon juice, garlic and parsley in a food processor or blender and process to combine. With machine running, pour in oil in a steady stream and process until thick. Season with black pepper to taste. Transfer to a serving bowl.
3. Arrange both steamed and fresh vegetables attractively on a large platter with aioli.

....
Serves 12

ingredients

> **250 g/8 oz asparagus, trimmed**
> **12 yellow baby squash**
> **125 g/4 oz green beans, trimmed**
> **12 baby potatoes**
> **12 button mushrooms**
> **12 cherry tomatoes**

parsley aioli

> **4 egg yolks**
> **2 teaspoons lemon juice**
> **4 cloves garlic**
> **2 tablespoons chopped fresh parsley**
> **1 cup/250 ml/8 fl oz olive oil**
> **freshly ground black pepper**

tip from the chef

Raw garlic has a strong taste. If you find this a problem, you might like to boil the garlic cloves (in their skin) before using. Garlic treated in this way has a milder flavor, which is preferred by some people, and will not linger as strongly on the breath.
To sweeten your breath after eating garlic, munch on some parsley.

ricotta
herb fettuccine

■□□ | Cooking time: 20 minutes - Preparation time: 10 minutes

ingredients
> **350 g/11 oz fettuccine**
> **155 g/5 oz ricotta cheese**
> **60 g/2 oz Pecorino cheese, grated**
> **30 g/1 oz butter**
> **1 tablespoon finely grated orange rind**
> **2 tablespoons snipped fresh chives**
> **2 tablespoons chopped fresh thyme**
> **2 tablespoons chopped fresh parsley**
> **freshly ground black pepper**

method
1. Cook pasta in boiling water in a large saucepan following packet directions. Drain and place in a bowl.
2. Combine ricotta cheese, Pecorino cheese, butter, orange rind, chives, thyme, parsley and black pepper to taste. Add ricotta mixture to pasta and toss to combine.
3. Spoon mixture into an 8-cup/2-liter/3 1/2-pt capacity ovenproof dish, cover with aluminum foil and bake at 180°C/350°F/Gas 4 for 8-10 minutes or until mixture is heated through.

....
Serves 4

tip from the chef
If you prefer a more creamy sauce, add 1/2 cup cream to the cottage cheese mixture.

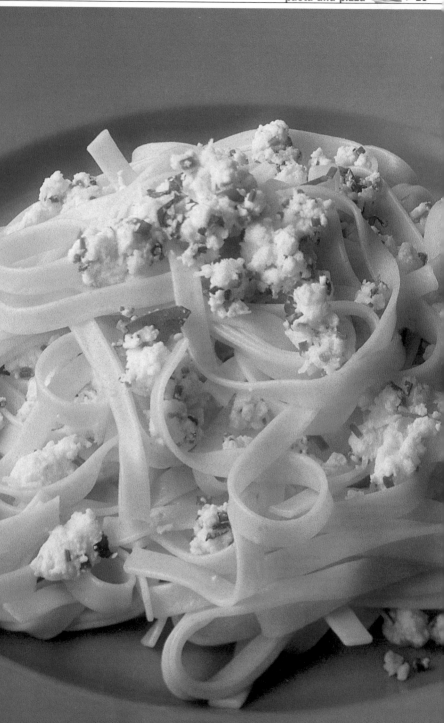

gnocchi
with herb sauce

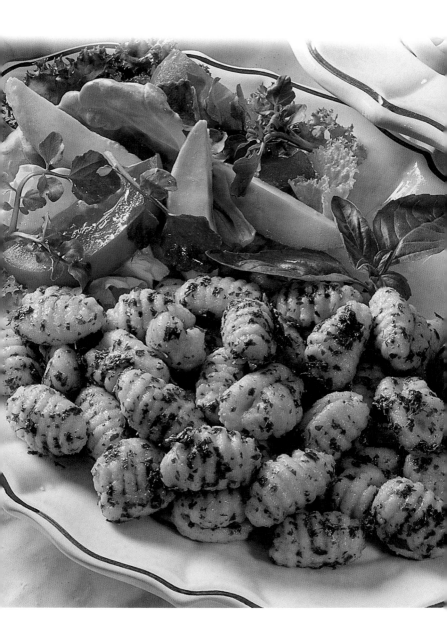

■□□ I Cooking time: 5 minutes - Preparation time: 15 minutes

method

1. Cook gnocchi in a large saucepan of boiling water following packet directions. Drain and keep warm.
2. To make sauce, place parsley, sage, basil, pine nuts and Parmesan cheese in a food processor or blender and process until combined. Add mayonnaise, stock and black pepper to taste and process until combined.
3. Spoon herb sauce over hot gnocchi and serve immediately.

Serves 4

ingredients

> 750 g/1¹/2 lb potato gnocchi

fresh herb sauce

> 2 tablespoons roughly chopped fresh parsley
> 2 tablespoons roughly chopped fresh sage
> 2 tablespoons roughly chopped fresh basil
> 2 tablespoons pine nuts
> 1 tablespoon grated Parmesan cheese
> 1 tablespoon mayonnaise
> 1 tablespoon vegetable stock
> freshly ground black pepper

tip from the chef

Accompany with steamed green vegetables of your choice or a salad and wholemeal bread rolls.

individual
oregano pizzas

■□□ I Cooking time: 15 minutes - Preparation time: 20 minutes

ingredients

quick pizza dough
> 4¹/₂ cups/560 g/
  1 lb 2 oz self-raising flour
> 1 tablespoon sugar
> 1 teaspoon salt
> 2 eggs, lightly beaten
> 1 cup/250 ml/8 fl oz
  olive oil
> ¹/₃ cup/90 ml/3 fl oz
  dry white wine

topping
> 4 tablespoons tomato
  paste (purée)
> 1 onion, thinly sliced
> 2 tomatoes, thinly sliced
> 1 tablespoon dried
  oregano
> freshly ground black
  pepper

method

1. To make dough, place flour, sugar and salt in a food processor and pulse once or twice to mix. With machine running, add eggs (a), then slowly pour in oil and wine. Continue processing until a smooth, glossy ball forms. Turn onto a lightly floured surface and knead briefly. Place in a bowl, cover and refrigerate until ready to use.
2. Divide dough into eight portions and roll each portion out to a 15 cm/6 in round (b). Place on lightly oiled baking trays.
3. To top pizza, spread each round with tomato paste (purée), then top with onion rings and tomato slices and sprinkle with oregano and black pepper to taste (c). Bake at 200°C/400°F/Gas 6 for 10-15 minutes or until dough is crisp and golden.

....
Makes 8

tip from the chef
The dough for these pizzas takes very little time to make, is easy to handle, and can be made in advance and stored in the refrigerator. Bring back to room temperature before using. If some of the oil separates during storage, knead dough to incorporate oil again before using.

a

b

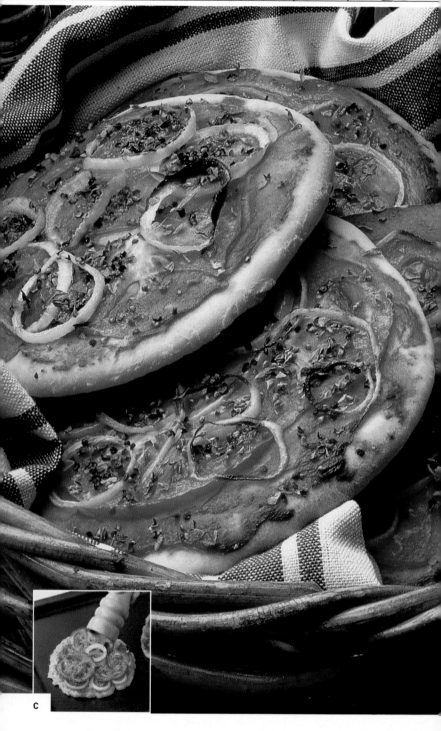

c

middle
eastern peppers

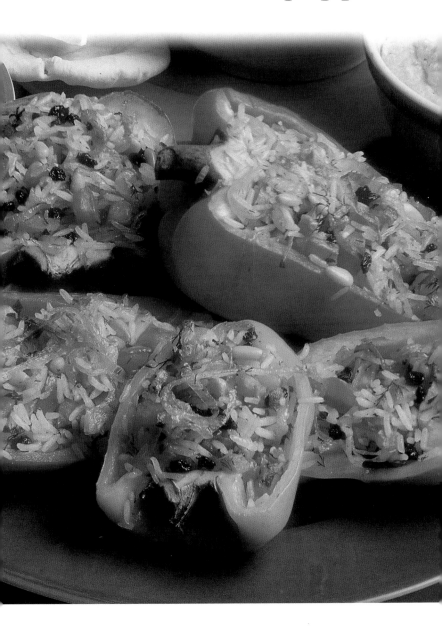

■□□ | Cooking time: 45 minutes - Preparation time: 15 minutes

method

1. Heat 2 tablespoons oil in a frying pan over a medium heat, add onions and sugar and cook, stirring, for 8 minutes or until sugar dissolves and onions are soft and caramelized.
2. Add rice, tomatoes (a), pine nuts, fennel leaves, currants and mint to pan and cook for 5 minutes.
3. Cut red, green and yellow peppers in half lengthwise and remove seeds and membranes. Place on a greased baking tray and brush peppers with a little oil (b).
4. Divide rice mixture between pepper shells (c) and bake at 180°C/350°F/Gas 4 for 30 minutes or until peppers are tender.

ingredients

> olive oil
> 3 onions, sliced
> 1 teaspoon sugar
> 1 cup/220 g/7 oz rice, cooked
> 2 tomatoes, chopped
> 2 tablespoons pine nuts, toasted
> 1 tablespoon chopped fresh fennel leaves
> 2 tablespoons currants
> 2 tablespoons chopped fresh mint
> 8 mixed red, green and yellow peppers

....
Serves 8

tip from the chef

Toasting pine nuts gives them a delicious flavor. The quickest method is to spread them in a thin layer on a baking tray, place under a preheated hot grill and toast until golden. Turn them several times during cooking to ensure all sides are toasted and to prevent burning. Set aside to cool.

a

b

c

quick
risotto milanese

■□□ | Cooking time: 12 minutes - Preparation time: 10 minutes

ingredients
> **60 g/2 oz butter**
> **1 onion, diced**
> **1 cup/220 g/7 oz long grain rice, washed and drained**
> **1 cup/250 ml/8 fl oz boiling chicken stock**
> **³/4 cup/185 ml/6 fl oz dry white wine**
> **1 teaspoon saffron powder**
> **60 g/2 oz Parmesan cheese, grated**

method
1. Place butter and onion in a microwavable bowl and cook on High (100%) for 2 minutes. Stir well.
2. Stir in rice, stock, wine and saffron, cover and cook for 10 minutes.
3. Stand for 4 minutes, stir in cheese and serve.

....
Serves 4

tip from the chef
Saffron originates from the stigmas of the saffron crocus flower which yields one of the most expensive spices. The stigmas must be harvested by hand and it takes 450.000 of them to make 1 kg/2 lb saffron. Patience is "the order of the day" when making a traditional risotto, but this microwave version is made in about half the time. Serve sprinkled with additional Parmesan cheese.

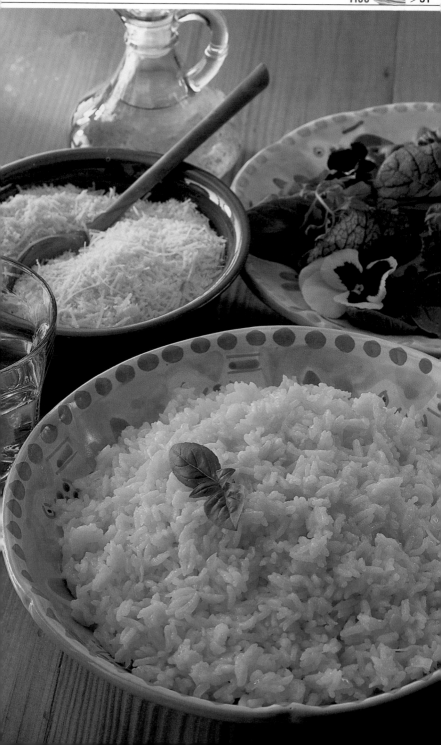

rice
and cheese triangles

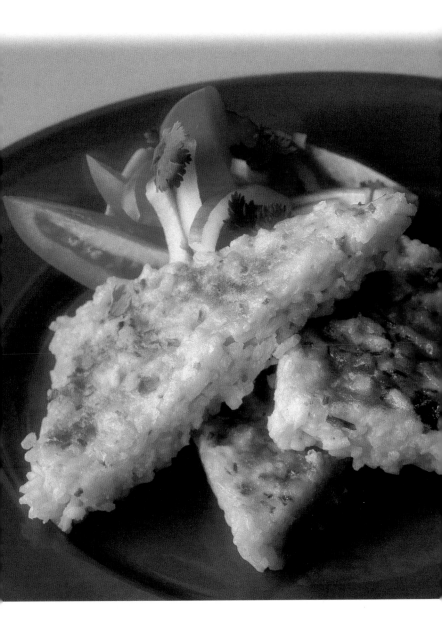

■□□ | Cooking time: 45 minutes - Preparation time: 15 minutes

method

1. Melt butter in a saucepan over a medium heat, add rice and cook, stirring constantly, for 4 minutes or until rice is translucent.
2. Add 1 cup/250 ml/8 fl oz hot stock (a) and cook, stirring constantly, until liquid is absorbed. Continue cooking in this way until all the stock is used and rice is a thick mixture that sticks together. Season to taste with black pepper.
3. Spread rice mixture over the base of a greased 26 x 32 cm/10½ x 12¾ in baking tray (b).
4. To make topping, place Gorgonzola, sour cream and chives in a bowl and mix to combine. Spread topping over rice (c) and bake at 180°C/350°F/Gas 4 for 20 minutes or until firm and golden. To serve, cut into large triangles.

ingredients

- > 30 g/1 oz butter
- > 2 cups/440 g/14 oz arborio rice
- > 4 cups/1 liter/1¾ pt hot vegetable stock
- > freshly ground black pepper

gorgonzola topping

- > 185 g/6 oz Gorgonzola cheese
- > ½ cup/125 g/4 oz sour cream
- > 3 tablespoons snipped fresh chives

....
Serves 4

tip from the chef

Any creamy soft blue cheese can be used to make this delicious dish.

a

b

c

peppered
salmon

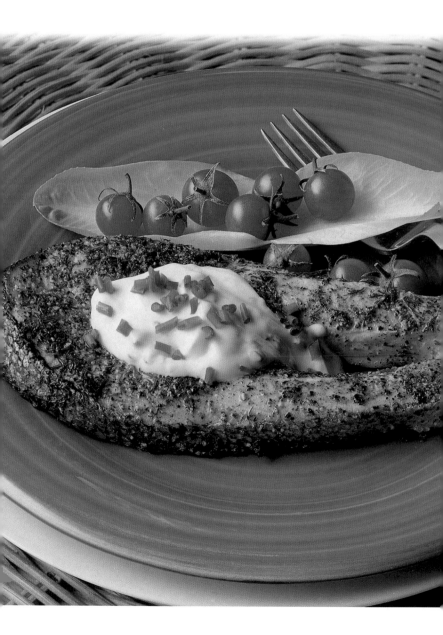

■□□ | Cooking time: 5 minutes - Preparation time: 15 minutes

method

1. To make lime yogurt, place chives, lime juice, lime rind, honey and yogurt in a bowl and mix well to combine. Cover and chill until required.
2. To make marinade, place black peppercorns, dill and lemon juice in a plastic food bag. Add salmon and shake to coat. Marinate for 5 minutes.
3. Melt butter in a frying pan over a medium heat, add salmon and cook for 2-3 minutes each side or until fish flakes when tested with a fork. Serve with lime yogurt.

Serves 4

ingredients

> **4 salmon cutlets**
> **30 g/1 oz butter**

black pepper marinade

> **2 tablespoons coarsely cracked black peppercorns**
> **2 tablespoons chopped fresh dill**
> **2 tablespoons lemon juice**

lime yogurt

> **2 tablespoons snipped fresh chives**
> **2 tablespoons lime juice**
> **1 tablespoon finely grated lime rind**
> **2 teaspoons honey**
> **1¹/4 cups/250 g/8 oz natural yogurt**

tip from the chef

Salmon is an oily fish which means that it has more omega-3 fatty acids than white fish such as sole, plaice or whiting. Medical research has shown that omega-3 has a lowering effect on blood pressure and blood fats. A salad of mixed lettuces tossed with balsamic or red wine vinegar is the perfect accompaniment for this dish.

grilled fish
with mandarin salsa

■□□ | Cooking time: 10 minutes - Preparation time: 15 minutes

ingredients
> **6 x 155 g/5 oz fish cutlets**
> **310 g/10 oz canned mandarin segments, drained and juice reserved**
> **30 g/1 oz butter**

coriander marinade
> **reserved mandarin juice**
> **3 tablespoons chopped fresh coriander**
> **3 tablespoons chopped fresh parsley**
> **1 teaspoon chili paste (sambal oelek)**
> **1/2 teaspoon ground cumin**
> **1/4 cup/60 ml/2 fl oz lime or lemon juice**
> **2 tablespoons white wine**

method
1. To make marinade, place mandarin juice, coriander, parsley, chili paste (sambal oelek), cumin, lime or lemon juice and wine in a bowl and mix to combine.
2. Place fish cutlets in a single layer in a shallow dish and pour marinade over. Cover and set aside to marinate for 1-2 hours. Drain fish and reserve marinade.
3. Cook fish cutlets on a preheated barbecue or under a preheated grill for 3-4 minutes each side or until flesh flakes when tested with a fork.
4. Place reserved marinade and mandarin segments in a small saucepan and bring to simmering. Remove saucepan from heat and stir in butter. Serve with fish.

....
Serves 6

tip from the chef
The combination of coriander and chili in this fish dish is reminiscent of Asian cuisine. Serve with boiled or steamed white or brown rice and a stir-fry of mixed vegetables.

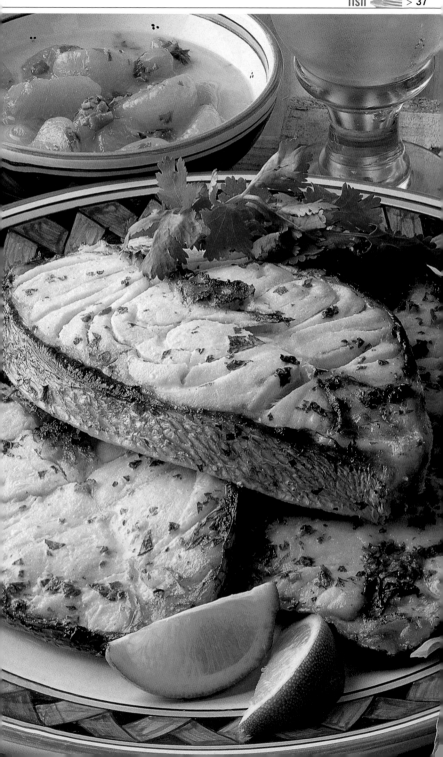

curried
fish cutlets

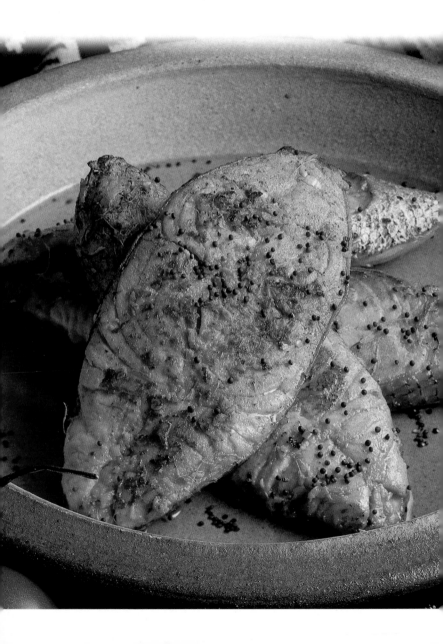

■□□ | Cooking time: 10 minutes - Preparation time: 10 minutes

method

1. Place ginger, garlic, chili powder and turmeric in a bowl and mix to combine. Add fish and toss to coat with chili mixture. Shake off any excess.

2. Heat oil in a nonstick frying pan over a medium heat, add fish and mustard seeds and cook for 5 minutes each side or until fish is golden and flesh flakes when tested with a fork. Serve immediately.

....

Serves 4

ingredients

- > **2 tablespoons finely grated fresh ginger**
- > **2 cloves garlic, crushed**
- > **1 teaspoon chili powder**
- > **1/2 teaspoon ground turmeric**
- > **4 cod or mackerel cutlets**
- > **2 tablespoons vegetable oil**
- > **2 tablespoons black mustard seeds**

tip from the chef

This dish can be made using any firm white fish cutlets or fillets.

tomato
chicken curry

■ ■ □ | Cooking time: 1 hour - Preparation time: 20 minutes

ingredients

> **2 tablespoons vegetable oil**
> **1 kg/2 lb chicken pieces**
> **1 onion, chopped**
> **3 cloves garlic, crushed**
> **2 tablespoons finely grated fresh ginger**
> **3 small fresh green chilies, chopped**
> **4 fresh or dried curry leaves**
> **2 tablespoons ground coriander**
> **1 tablespoon ground cumin**
> **1 teaspoon ground turmeric**
> **1 tablespoon black mustard seeds**
> **440 g/14 oz canned tomatoes, undrained and mashed**
> **1¹/2 cups/375 ml/ 12 fl oz coconut milk**

method

1. Heat oil in a saucepan over a medium heat, add chicken and cook, turning frequently, for 10 minutes or until brown on all sides. Remove chicken from pan and set aside.
2. Add onion and garlic to pan and cook, stirring, for 3 minutes or until onion is soft. Stir in ginger, chilies, curry leaves, coriander, cumin, turmeric and mustard seeds and cook for 2 minutes longer or until fragrant.
3. Stir in tomatoes and coconut milk and return chicken to pan. Bring to simmering and simmer, stirring occasionally, for 45 minutes or until chicken is tender.

....
Serves 6

tip from the chef
Curry leaves are available fresh or dried from Oriental and Indian food shops.

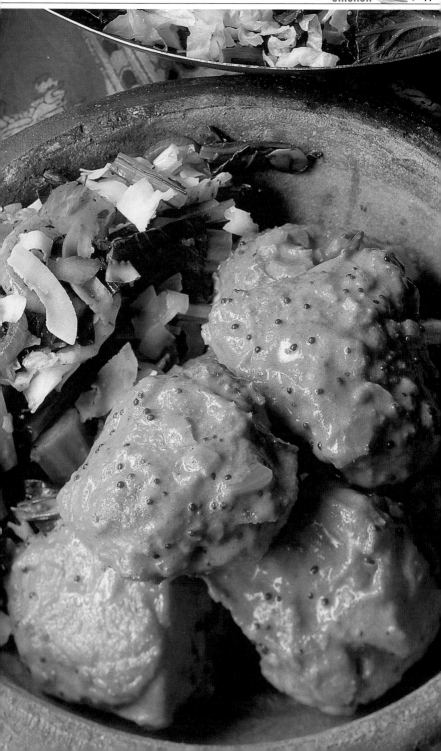

thai
curry chicken salad

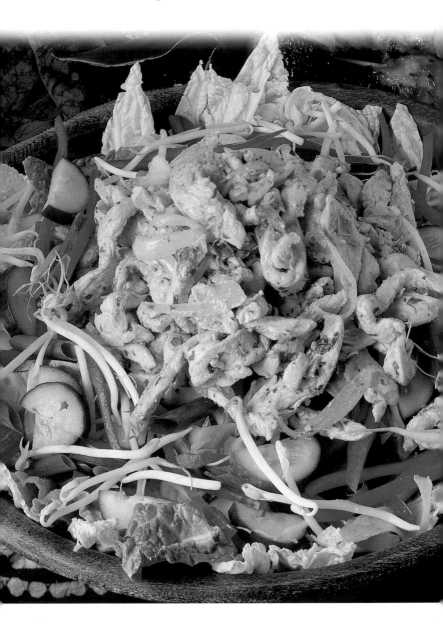

■□□ | Cooking time: 15 minutes - Preparation time: 10 minutes

method

1. Heat oil in a wok over a medium heat, add garlic, ginger, chilies, lemon grass, lime rind and onion and stir-fry for 4-5 minutes or until onion is golden.

2. Stir chicken, fish sauce and sugar into pan and cook, stirring frequently, for 10 minutes or until chicken is tender. Remove pan from heat and set aside to cool slightly. Add mint and coriander and toss to combine.

3. To serve, line a large platter with cabbage, then top with spring onions, cucumbers, bean sprouts, red pepper and chicken mixture.

Serves 4

ingredients

> 1 tablespoon sesame oil
> 1 clove garlic, crushed
> 1 tablespoon finely grated fresh ginger
> 2 small fresh red chilies, finely chopped
> 1 stalk lemon grass, chopped, or 1/2 teaspoon dried lemon grass, soaked
> 1/2 teaspoon grated lime rind
> 1 onion, cut in wedges
> 500 g/1 lb boneless chicken breast fillets, thinly sliced
> 1 tablespoon Thai fish sauce (nam pla)
> 1 tablespoon sugar
> 2 tablespoons chopped fresh mint
> 1 tablespoon chopped fresh coriander
> 1 Chinese cabbage, sliced
> 3 spring onions, sliced
> 2 cucumbers, sliced
> 125 g/4 oz bean sprouts
> 1 red pepper, thinly sliced

tip from the chef

Fish sauce "nam pla" is characteristic of Thai cooking and appears as a seasoning in many dishes. Thai cooks take pride in making their own fish sauce and the ability to make a good sauce is the hallmark of an accomplished housewife.

chicken
curry with spiced lentils

■□□ | Cooking time: 35 minutes - Preparation time: 15 minutes

ingredients

> **2 teaspoons oil**
> **2 cloves garlic, crushed**
> **1 teaspoon ground coriander**
> **1/2 teaspoon ground turmeric**
> **1/2 teaspoon ground cardamom**
> **3 boneless chicken breast fillets, sliced**
> **2 cups/500 ml/16 fl oz chicken stock**
> **11/4 cups/315 ml/10 fl oz coconut milk**
> **6 potatoes, chopped**
> **1 red pepper, chopped**
> **2 teaspoons garam masala**

spiced lentils

> **2 teaspoons oil**
> **2 fresh green chilies, chopped**
> **1 tablespoon grated fresh ginger**
> **1 tablespoon yellow mustard seeds**
> **1 tablespoon ground cumin**
> **3 tablespoons chopped fresh coriander**
> **500 g/1 lb green lentils, cooked**
> **1/2 cup/125 ml/4 fl oz vegetable stock**
> **1/2 cup/100 g/31/2 oz natural yogurt**

method

1. Heat oil in a saucepan over a medium heat, add garlic, coriander, turmeric and cardamom and cook, stirring, for 2 minutes. Add chicken and cook, stirring, for 4 minutes or until brown.

2. Add stock, coconut milk, potatoes and red pepper and mix to combine. Bring to the boil, then reduce heat and simmer for 20 minutes or until potatoes are tender and curry thickens. Stir in garam marsala.

3. To make lentils, heat oil in a frying pan over a medium heat, add chilies, ginger, mustard seeds, cumin and coriander and cook, stirring, for 2 minutes.

4. Add lentils and stock and cook for 5 minutes longer or until stock is absorbed. Serve with yogurt.

....
Serves 6

tip from the chef

This curry can be made the day before and reheated when required. You may like to include slices of cucumber with the yogurt which accompanies this dish to cool the heat of the seasoning.

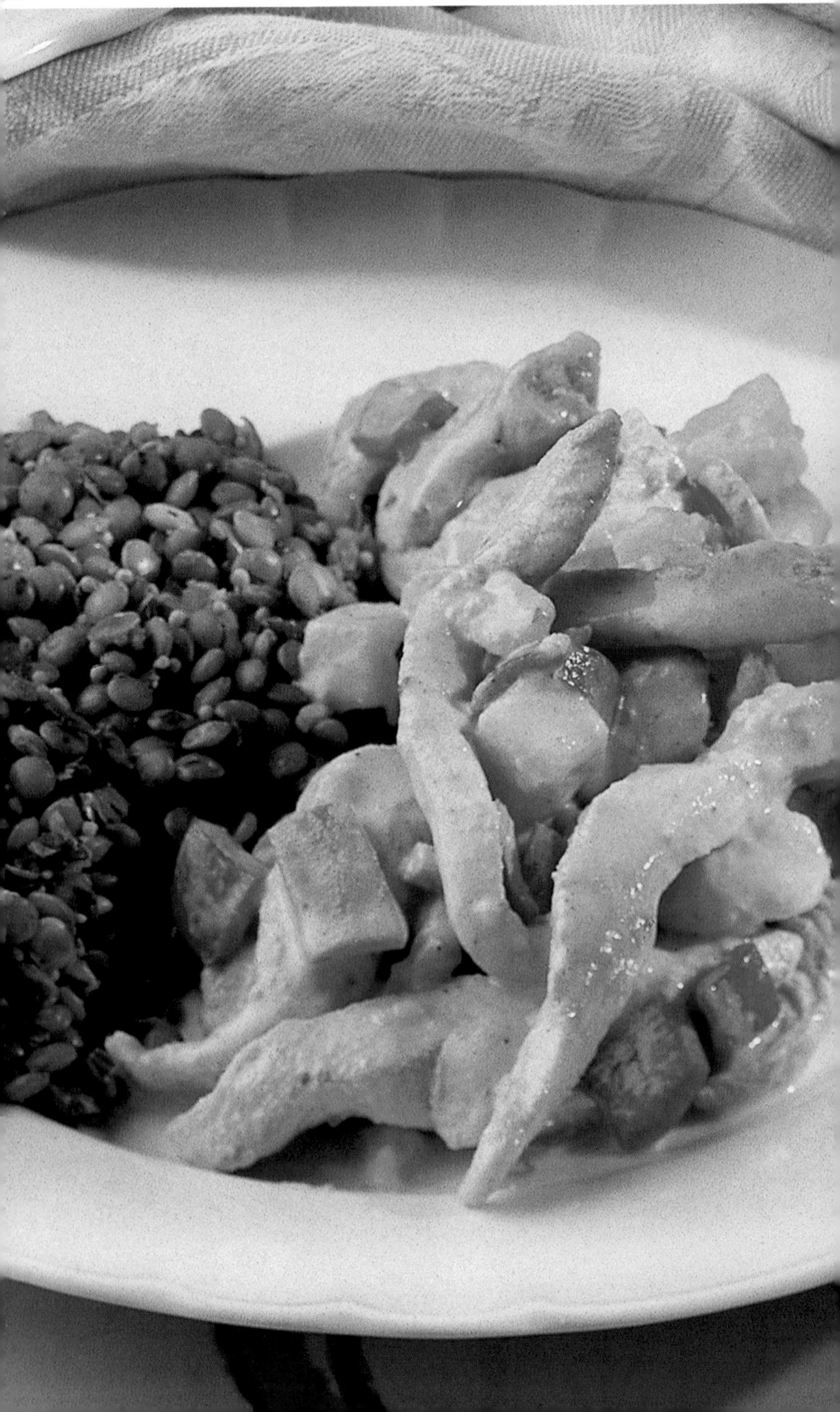

herbed
chicken en papillote

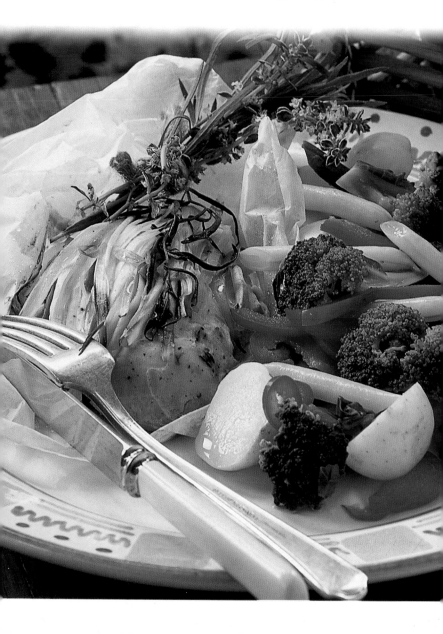

■ ■ □ | Cooking time: 30 minutes - Preparation time: 20 minutes

method

1. Place thyme, mint, vinegar, yogurt and black pepper to taste in a shallow glass or ceramic dish and mix to combine. Add chicken, turn to coat, cover and marinate in the refrigerator for 3 hours.
2. Cut 4 circles of nonstick baking paper large enough to completely enclose fillets. The paper should be at least 10 cm/4 in larger than fillets on all sides. Fold paper in half lengthwise and cut a half-heart shape.
3. Open out paper hearts and place equal amounts of leek on one half of each heart near the center fold line. Drain chicken and place on top of leeks. Add a sprig of tarragon, fold other half of paper over ingredients and roll edges to seal.
4. Place paper parcels on a baking tray and bake at 180°C/350°F/Gas 4 for 30 minutes or until chicken is tender.

ingredients

> 1 tablespoon chopped fresh thyme
> 1 tablespoon chopped fresh mint
> 2 teaspoons tarragon vinegar
> 2 tablespoons natural yogurt
> freshly ground black pepper
> 4 boneless chicken breast fillets
> 1 leek, cut into thin strips
> 4 sprigs fresh tarragon

....
Serves 4

tip from the chef

Part of the fun of this dish is serving it at the table still wrapped and allowing each person to enjoy the wonderful aromas that are released when the parcel is opened.

javanese
beef

■ □ □ | Cooking time: 30 minutes - Preparation time: 15 minutes

ingredients

> **vegetable oil
for deep-frying**
> **750 g/1 1/2 lb chuck
steak, cut into 2 cm/
3/4 in cubes**
> **1 large onion, chopped**
> **3 cloves garlic, crushed**
> **1/2 cup/125 ml/4 fl oz
kechap manis**
> **2 teaspoons chili paste
(sambal oelek)**
> **1 cup/250 ml/8 fl oz
coconut milk**
> **1 tablespoon lime juice**
> **2 tablespoons fresh
coconut shavings**

method

1. Heat oil in a large saucepan until a cube
   of bread dropped in browns in 50 seconds.
   Add beef and deep-fry for 5 minutes
   or until brown. Remove beef from oil
   and drain on absorbent kitchen paper.
2. Heat 1 tablespoon oil in a frying pan over
   a medium heat, add onion and garlic and
   stir-fry for 3 minutes or until onion is soft.
3. Stir in kechap manis, chili paste (sambal
   oelek), coconut milk and lime juice and
   bring to simmering. Simmer, stirring
   occasionally, for 15 minutes or until
   mixture thickens slightly.
4. Return beef to pan and cook for 5 minutes
   longer or until heated through. Sprinkle
   with coconut shavings and serve.

....
Serves 6

tip from the chef

*Coconut milk can be purchased in a number
of forms: canned, or as a long-life product
in cartons, or as a powder to which you add
water. Once opened it has a short life and
should be used within a day or so. It is
available from Oriental food stores and some
supermarkets.*

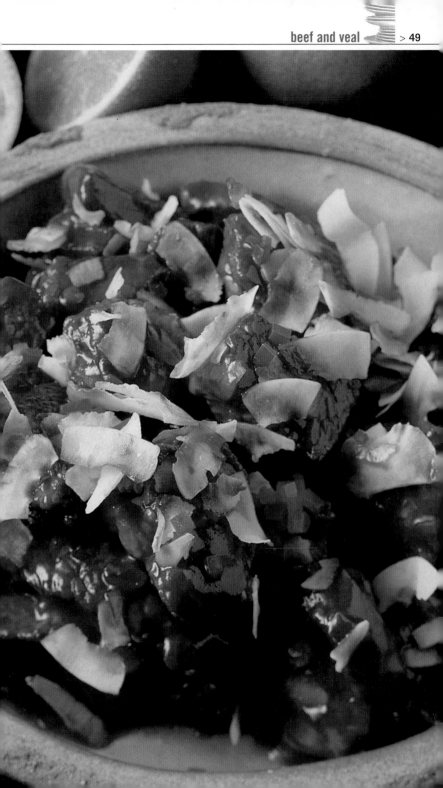

mustard-crusted
steaks

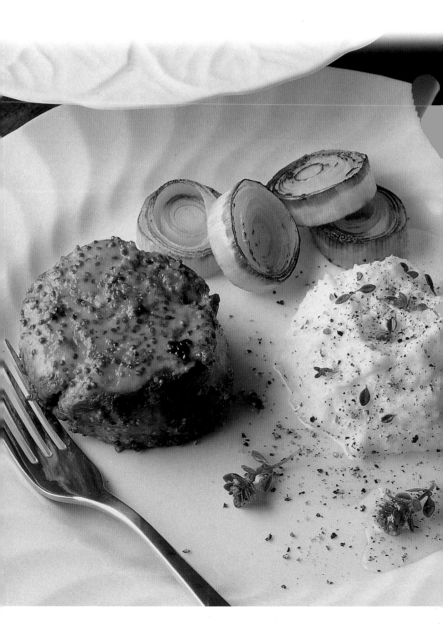

■□□ | Cooking time: 5 minutes - Preparation time: 10 minutes

method

1. To make crust, place mustard, garlic, honey and mayonnaise in a small bowl and mix to combine. Spread mustard mixture over steaks.
2. Heat oil in a frying pan over a high heat, add steaks and cook for 2 minutes each side or until cooked to your liking.

Serves 4

ingredients

> **4 lean beef fillet steaks**
> **2 teaspoons vegetable oil**

mustard crust

> **4 tablespoons wholegrain mustard**
> **1 clove garlic, crushed**
> **1 tablespoon honey**
> **2 tablespoons mayonnaise**

tip from the chef

An unusual accompaniment is broccoli with browned garlic. To make, divide a large head of broccoli into small flowerets, then boil, steam or microwave it until just tender. Refresh under cold running water. Divide a head of garlic into individual cloves and peel each clove. Heat 3 tablespoons olive oil in a frying pan, add garlic and cook, stirring, for 5-7 minutes or until brown. Take care that the garlic does not burn. Add broccoli to pan and cook, stirring, for 2-3 minutes or until heated. To complete the meal add mashed potatoes and sprinkle with fresh thyme.

herb
schnitzels

■□□ | Cooking time: 10 minutes - Preparation time: 20 minutes

ingredients

- > **4 lean veal schnitzels**
- > **1/4 cup/60 ml/2 fl oz lemon juice**
- > **1/4 cup/60 ml/2 fl oz dry vermouth**
- > **3 tablespoons vegetable oil**
- > **3/4 cup/90 g/3 oz dried breadcrumbs**
- > **1 tablespoon chopped fresh rosemary**
- > **1 tablespoon chopped fresh parsley**
- > **flour to coat**
- > **1 egg, lightly beaten**
- > **30 g/1 oz butter**
- > **2 teaspoons cornflour blended with 1/2 cup/ 125 ml/4 fl oz cream**

method

1. Trim veal of all visible fat and place in a shallow dish. Combine lemon juice, vermouth and 2 tablespoons oil. Pour over veal and set aside to marinate for 10-15 minutes.

2. Drain meat and reserve marinade. Combine breadcrumbs, rosemary and parsley and place in a shallow dish. Place flour in a plastic food bag, add veal and shake to coat (a). Shake excess flour from veal, then dip in egg and coat with breadcrumb mixture (b).

3. Heat butter and 1 tablespoon oil in a frying pan and cook veal (c) for 2-3 minutes each side or until golden. Remove from pan, set aside and keep warm.

4. Drain pan of excess fat and pour in reserved marinade. Bring to the boil and boil until liquid has reduced by half, whisk in cornflour mixture and cook, stirring, until sauce thickens. Spoon sauce over veal and serve immediately.

....

Serves 4

tip from the chef

For something different you might like to replace the rosemary in this recipe with thyme, oregano or marjoram. Serve these tasty schnitzels with a stir-fry of leeks, mushrooms and pumpkin or carrot, or a tossed green salad and baked potatoes.

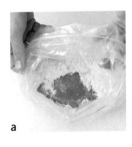

a

b

c

spicy lamb curry

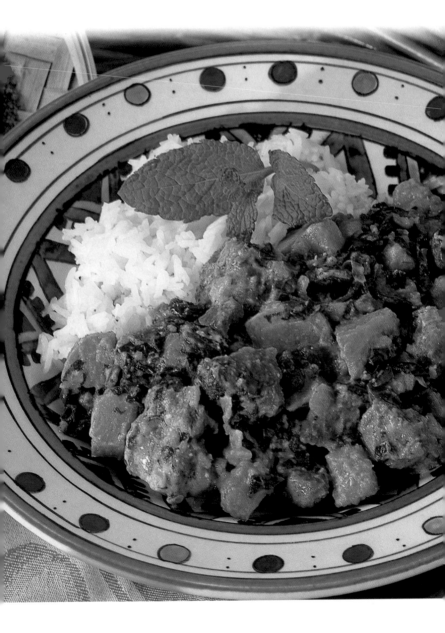

■□□ | Cooking time: 50 minutes - Preparation time: 20 minutes

method

1. Heat oil in a saucepan over a medium heat, add onion, garlic and ginger and cook, stirring, for 3 minutes or until onion is golden. Stir in curry paste, turmeric and coriander and cook, stirring, for 3 minutes or until fragrant. Add lamb and cook, stirring, for 5 minutes or until brown.

2. Add potatoes, sweet potato and stock or water, bring to simmering and simmer, stirring occasionally, for 30 minutes. Add spinach, sultanas and mint and cook for 10 minutes longer or until lamb is tender.

3. Remove pan from heat, stir in yogurt and serve immediately.

Serves 6

ingredients

> 1 tablespoon vegetable oil
> 1 onion, diced
> 1 clove garlic, crushed
> 2.5 cm/1 in piece fresh ginger, roughly chopped
> 1 tablespoon red curry paste
> 1 teaspoon ground turmeric
> 1 tablespoon ground coriander
> 500 g/1 lb lean lamb, trimmed of all visible fat and cut into 2.5 cm/1 in cubes
> 6 small potatoes, halved
> 315 g/10 oz sweet potato, chopped
> 1 cup/250 ml/8 fl oz stock
> 1 bunch English spinach, shredded
> 60 g/2 oz sultanas
> 2 tablespoons chopped fresh mint
> 1 cup/200 g/6^1/$_2$ oz natural yogurt

tip from the chef

Red curry paste is available from Oriental food stores and some supermarkets. If it is unavailable any curry paste can be used but you may need to adjust the quantity used depending on the hotness of the paste.

lamb
with mustard herb crust

■■□ | Cooking time: 30 minutes - Preparation time: 20 minutes

ingredients

> 2 racks baby lamb,
  6 chops each
> 1 cup fresh white
  breadcrumbs
> 1/2 cup finely chopped
  fresh parsley
> 1/4 cup finely chopped
  fresh rosemary
> 1 clove garlic, crushed
> 2 tablespoons Dijon
  mustard
> 2 tablespoons olive oil

method

1. Trim rack of lamb, leaving the rib bones as long as possible. Leave about 5 mm/ 1/4 in of fat on the outside of the rack.
2. In a small bowl, combine breadcrumbs, parsley, rosemary, garlic, mustard and olive oil. Set aside.
3. Place racks of lamb in a baking dish and cook for 15 minutes in a moderate oven. Remove from oven.
4. Press the breadcrumbs mixture on top of the rack to form a crust. Return to the oven for another 10-15 minutes.

....
Serves 4

tip from the chef

Steamed pumpkin and broccoli are a good side dish, the same as potatoes, sweet potatoes, carrots and onions baked along with lamb.

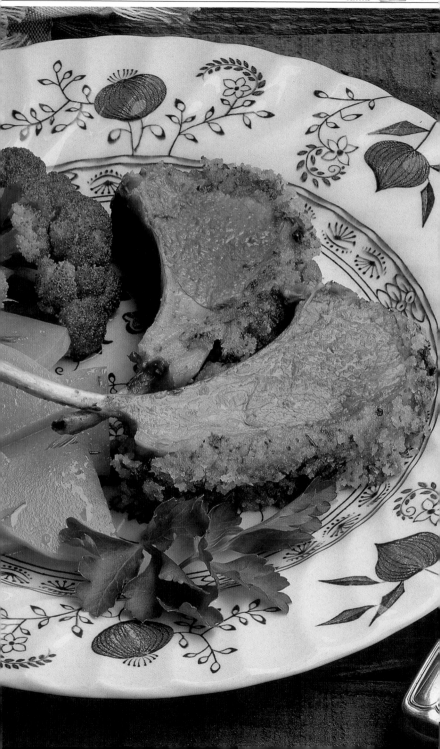

fiery
lamb curry

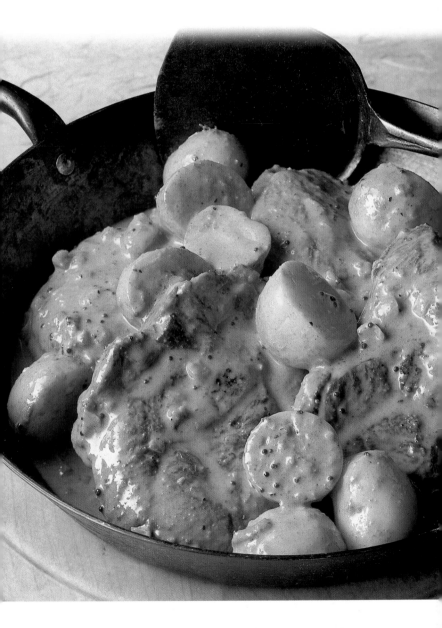

■ ■ □ | Cooking time: 55 minutes - Preparation time: 20 minutes

method

1. Place onion, garlic and ginger into a food processor or blender and process to finely chop.

2. Melt ghee or butter in a large nonstick frying pan over a medium heat, add onion mixture and cook, stirring, for 2 minutes or until mixture is golden. Stir in coriander, cumin, black pepper, turmeric, mustard seeds and chili powder and cook for 2 minutes longer or until fragrant.

3. Add chops and cook for 5 minutes on each side or until brown. Add potatoes, sultanas, coconut milk, mint and cinnamon, bring to simmering and simmer, stirring occasionally, for 40 minutes or until chops are tender.

....

Serves 4

ingredients

> 1 onion, roughly chopped
> 2 cloves garlic, chopped
> 2.5 cm/1 in piece fresh ginger, roughly chopped
> 30 g/1 oz ghee or butter
> 1 teaspoon ground coriander
> 1 teaspoon ground cumin
> 1 teaspoon freshly ground black pepper
> 1 teaspoon ground turmeric
> 1 teaspoon black mustard seeds, crushed
> 1 teaspoon chili powder
> 500 g/1 lb lamb chops, trimmed of all visible fat
> 6 small new potatoes, halved
> 90 g/3 oz sultanas
> 1 1/2 cups/375 ml/ 12 fl oz coconut milk
> 2 tablespoons chopped fresh mint
> 1 cinnamon stick

tip from the chef

Ghee is a form of clarified butter used extensively in Asian cooking.

fruity
pork salad

■ ■ □ | Cooking time: 25 minutes - Preparation time: 20 minutes

ingredients

> 15 g/¹/2 oz butter
> 1 tablespoon vegetable oil
> 1.5 kg/3 lb pork fillets
> 90 g/3 oz sultanas
> 3 spring onions, cut diagonally into 2 cm/ ³/4 in pieces
> 3 large green apples, cored and cut into 2 cm/³/4 in cubes
> 60 g/2 oz dried apricots, chopped and soaked
> 185 g/6 oz pitted prunes, soaked

parsley dressing

> ¹/2 cup/125 ml/4 fl oz olive oil
> 2 tablespoons lemon juice
> 2 tablespoons vinegar
> 1 tablespoon French mustard
> 2 teaspoons brown sugar
> 2 tablespoons chopped fresh parsley
> freshly ground black pepper

method

1. Heat butter and oil in a frying pan and cook pork fillets over a high heat until brown on all sides (a).
2. Transfer pork to a baking dish and bake for 15 minutes or until cooked. Remove from dish and set aside to cool. Reserve pan juices.
3. Heat reserved pan juices in frying pan and cook sultanas, spring onions and apples over a medium heat for 5 minutes or until apples are soft. Transfer to a large bowl. Add apricots and prunes (b). Cut pork into slices (c) and add to fruit mixture.
4. To make dressing, place olive oil, lemon juice, vinegar, mustard, sugar, parsley and black pepper to taste in a screwtop jar and shake well to combine. Pour over salad and toss to combine.

....
Serves 8

tip from the chef

While parsley is probably the best known and most used herb, its exact origin is unknown. It is thought to have come from Sardinia and was used by the ancient Greeks and Romans. The Romans made garlands of parsley for banquet guests and ate large quantities in an attempt to prevent drunkenness!

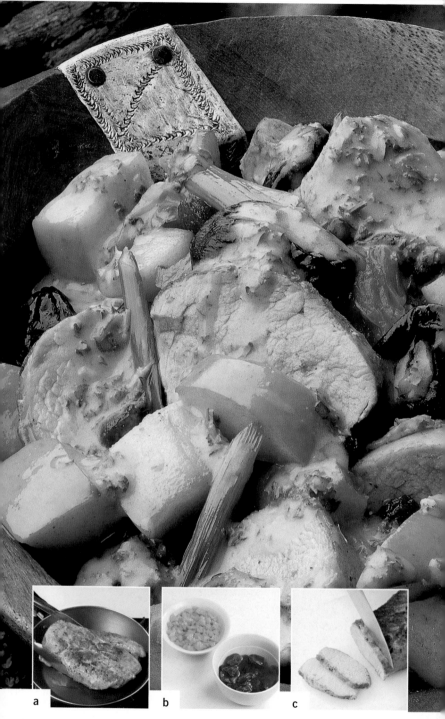

a

b

c

pork
and mango curry

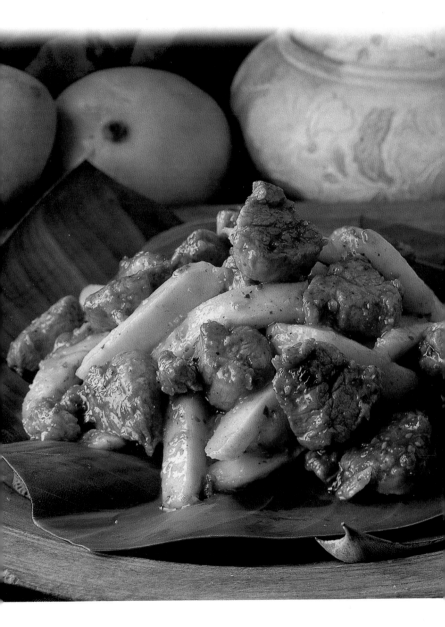

■□□ | Cooking time: 35 minutes - Preparation time: 15 minutes

method

1. Place onion, garlic, chilies, coriander, cumin, fennel and fenugreek seeds, cinnamon and cloves into food processor or blender and process to make a smooth paste.

2. Heat sesame and vegetable oils together in a wok over a medium heat, add paste and stir-fry for 5 minutes or until all the liquid evaporates.

3. Add pork and stir-fry for 10 minutes or until pork is brown. Add lemon grass, fish sauce and lemon juice and cook over a low heat, stirring frequently, for 15 minutes or until all the liquid evaporates. Stir in mangoes and chutney and cook for 2-3 minutes longer or until heated through.

....
Serves 6

ingredients

> 1 large onion, chopped
> 4 cloves garlic, chopped
> 2 small fresh red chilies, chopped
> 2 teaspoons coriander seeds
> 1 teaspoon cumin seeds
> 1/2 teaspoon fennel seeds
> 1/2 teaspoon fenugreek seeds
> 1/4 teaspoon ground cinnamon
> 1/4 teaspoon ground cloves
> 1 tablespoon sesame oil
> 1 tablespoon vegetable oil
> 1 kg/2 lb pork fillets, cut into 2 cm/3/4 in wide strips
> 2 stalks fresh lemon grass, chopped, or 1 teaspoon dried lemon grass, soaked
> 1 tablespoon Thai fish sauce (nam pla)
> 2 tablespoons lemon juice
> 2 mangoes, stoned, peeled and sliced
> 3 tablespoons mango chutney

tip from the chef
Some prefer to seed chilies so that they do not taste so pungent.

index

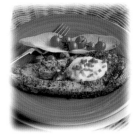